IN THE AIR!

written by Claire Philip

Illustrated by Maxine Lee-Mackie

Miles Kelly

Let's fly!

Every day, planes of different sizes carry people and cargo around the world.

Airport terminal
I can carry more than 400 passengers!
It costs more to fly on a business jet than a normal plane, as passengers hire the whole plane!
Passenger planes take people on journeys for holiday or work.
Runway
I zoom along the runway to gather enough speed to take off!

Super-sized

This Airbus A380 is currently the biggest airliner in the world!

With two levels of seating for its passengers, the Airbus A380 is like a massive double-decker bus.

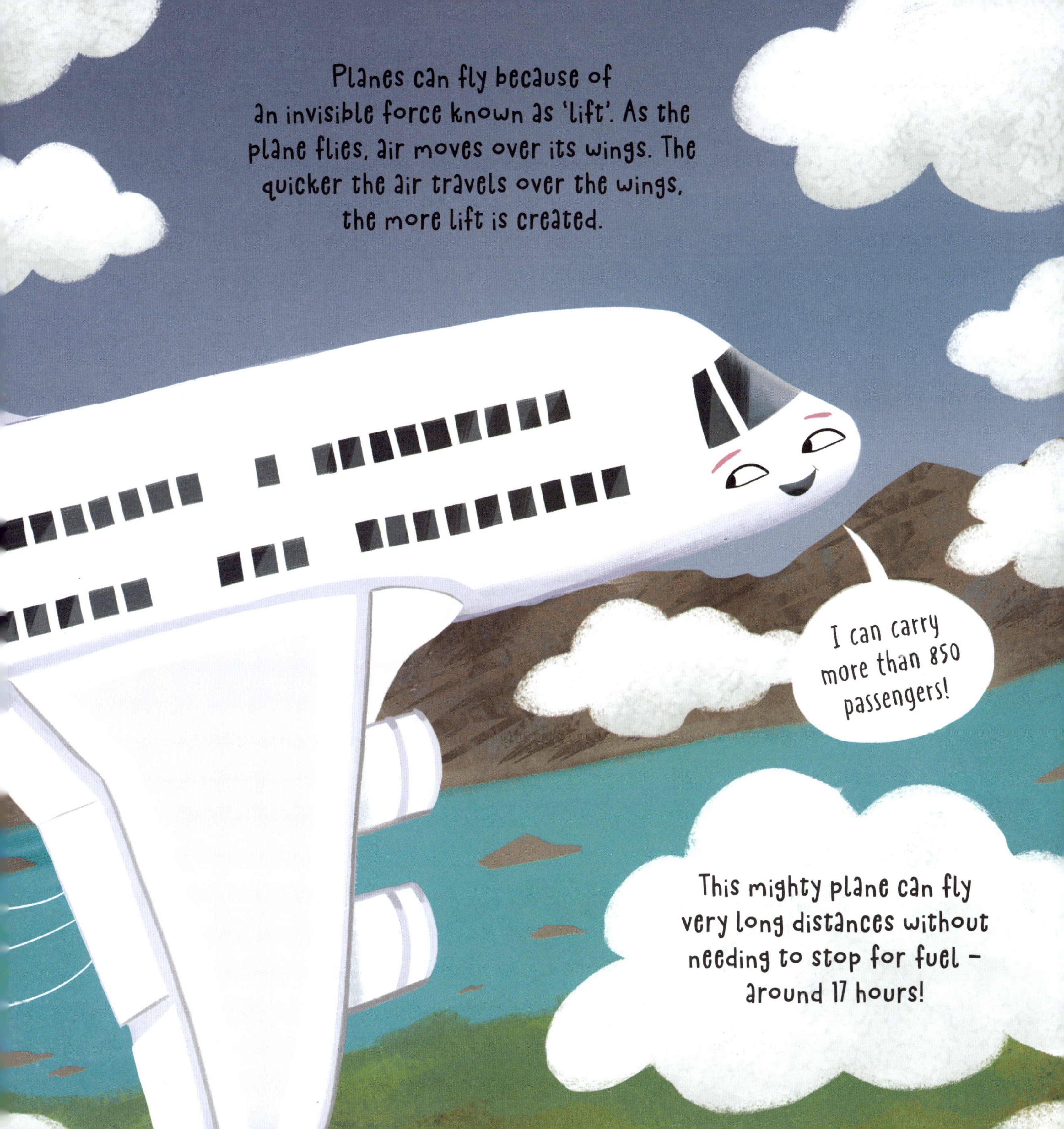
Planes can fly because of an invisible force known as 'lift'. As the plane flies, air moves over its wings. The quicker the air travels over the wings, the more lift is created.
I can carry more than 850 passengers!
This mighty plane can fly very long distances without needing to stop for fuel – around 17 hours!

Propeller power!

Propellers help aircraft move forward by creating a force called thrust. They are powered by a plane's engine.

Most planes today are monoplanes, meaning they only have one set of wings.

Biplanes have two sets of wings, while triplanes have three.
Biplane
These planes can perform spectacular stunts!
Triplane
Planes powered by propellers use less fuel, but they're slower than jet planes.
My wings are stacked on top of one another!

Landing on water

Splash! Did you know that some planes can land on, and take off from, water?

Floatplanes are used to get to remote islands that don't have space for long runways.

These planes don't have wheels. Instead, they have two floats that rest on the water's surface.

If the weather is stormy, floatplanes can't fly – it would be too dangerous to try and land on choppy waters.
Welcome aboard!
The main body of the plane, called the fuselage, doesn't touch the water.

In an emergency

Many emergency services are air-based as they can get to locations very quickly.

In some places, wildfires are common. Special fire-fighting tanker planes fly over the flames and drop huge amounts of water.

Air ambulance helicopters can quickly reach people in rural or remote places.

Coastguard helicopters rescue people in danger at sea. If someone needs lifting from the water, they can be pulled up using a mechanism called a winch.

High fliers

There are lots of ways to take to the sky. How many of these have you seen?

Light sport aircraft

Wing suit

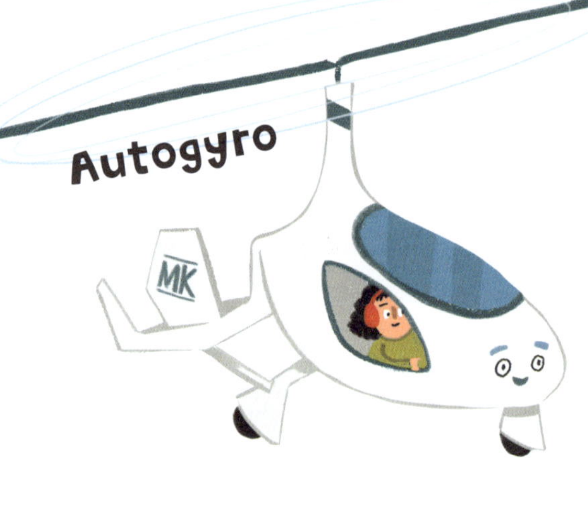

Autogyro

Microlight

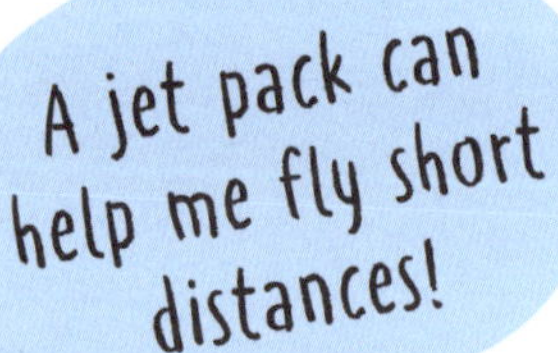

Jet pack

Gyrodyne

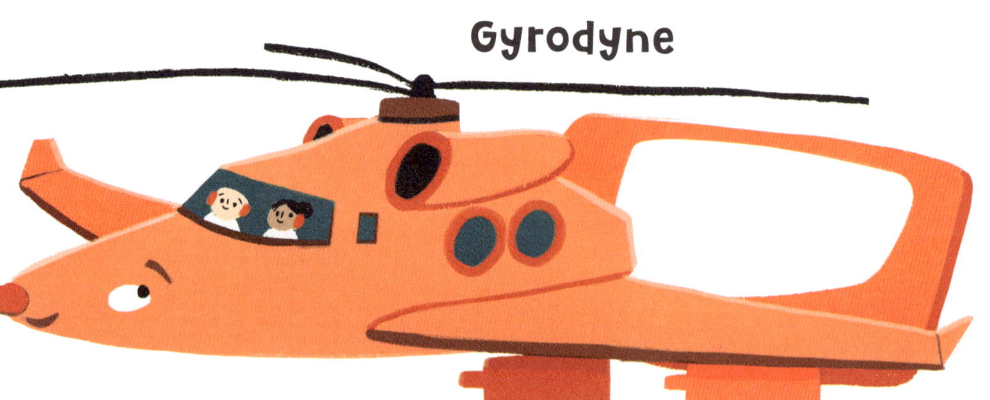

Tilt rotor plane
Ultralight
Motor glider
Watch us perform amazing stunts in the sky!
Turboprop plane
Flyboard
Aerobatic display planes
Blended wing plane

Future of flight!

Technology is helping to make planes quieter and kinder to the environment. New types of aircraft are being invented all the time.

X-59

Supersonic passenger planes, like the X-59, can fly at twice the speed of sound!

Solar Impulse 2 was the first plane to fly around the world completely powered by the sun!

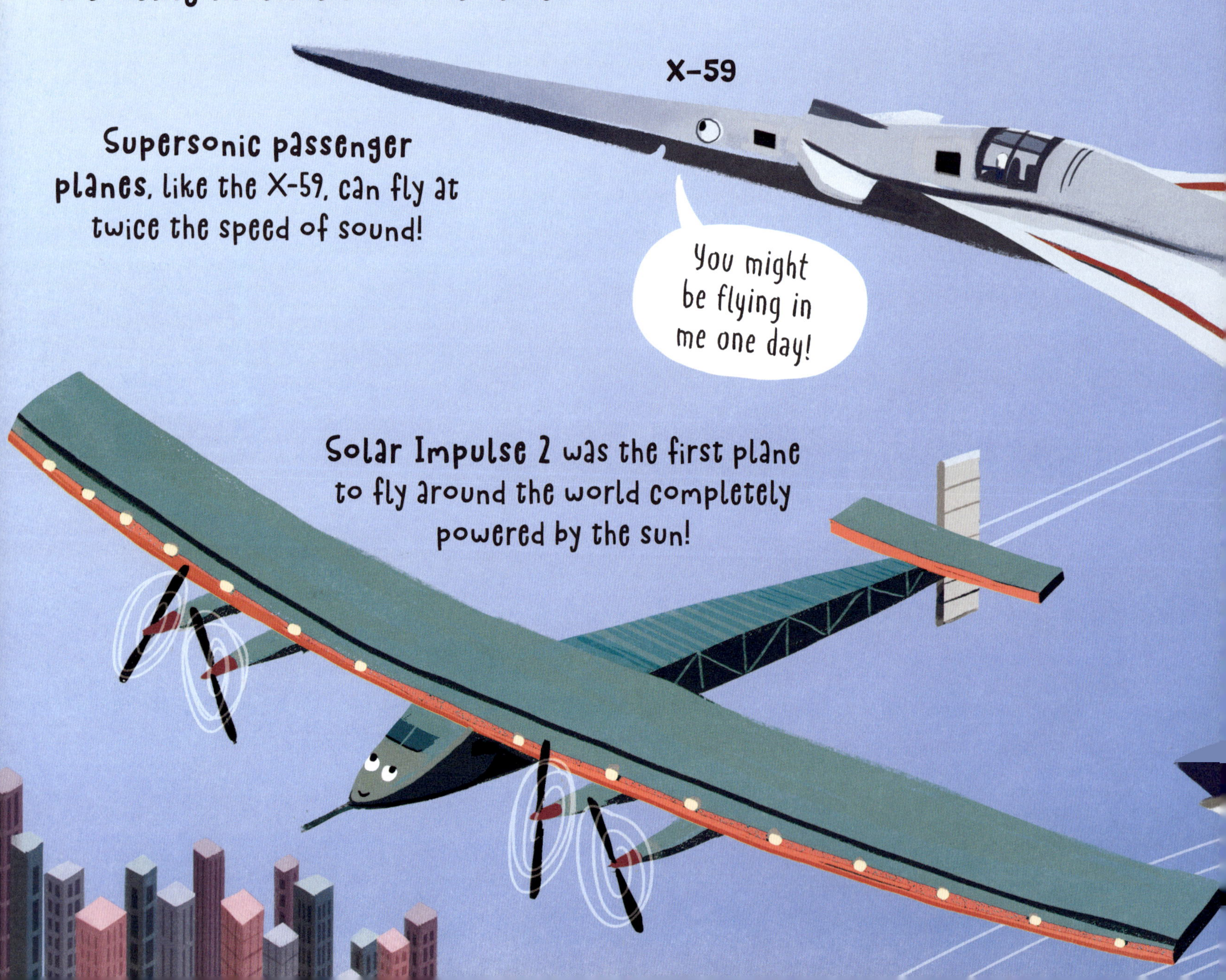

The small plane Elektra One Solar uses a mixture of electricity and solar energy to fly.

Fancy a holiday in space? Craft like the VSS Unity are being built to take tourists on short flights way above Earth.

Lift up and off!

Whomp! Whomp! Helicopters have spinning blades called rotors that lift them off the ground!

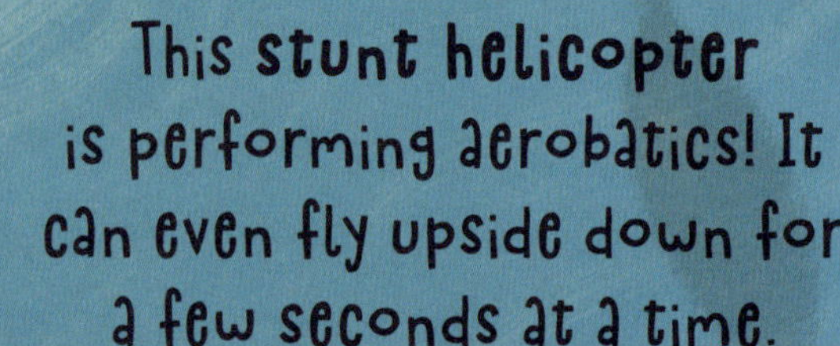

This **stunt helicopter** is performing aerobatics! It can even fly upside down for a few seconds at a time.

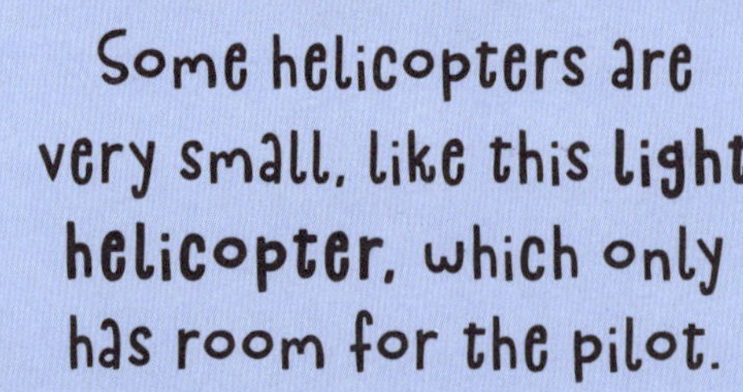

Some helicopters are very small, like this **light helicopter**, which only has room for the pilot.

Is that a flying crane?
No! It's a helicopter! This
powerful **skycrane** can carry
super-heavy loads.

A twin-rotor helicopter
has two rotors, which gives
it extra lifting power.

up and away!

Which aircraft can fly without an engine? A sailplane!

An engine-powered plane tows the **sailplane** up into the sky. Then it is released to glide and soar on the air!

Hang-gliders set off from high places, such as hillsides, then the pilot glides to the ground using a control bar to steer.

Lighter than air

Hot air balloons make use of the fact that warm air is lighter than cool air.

To take off, the pilot turns on the burner to heat up the air inside the hot air balloon.

Once the air inside the balloon is warmer than the air outside, the balloon lifts!

To come back down,
the pilot slowly lets air
out of the balloon.

I make
almost no
noise!

The passengers stand with
the pilot in the balloon's
basket. This is also where
the fuel is kept.

All about airships!

Sometimes called zeppelins or blimps, airships are filled with a gas called helium.

Unlike a hot air balloon, an airship is engine powered. The pilot uses a rudder to steer it.

To come down, the pilot pumps air, which is heavier than helium, into the main body of the airship – and slowly it sinks!

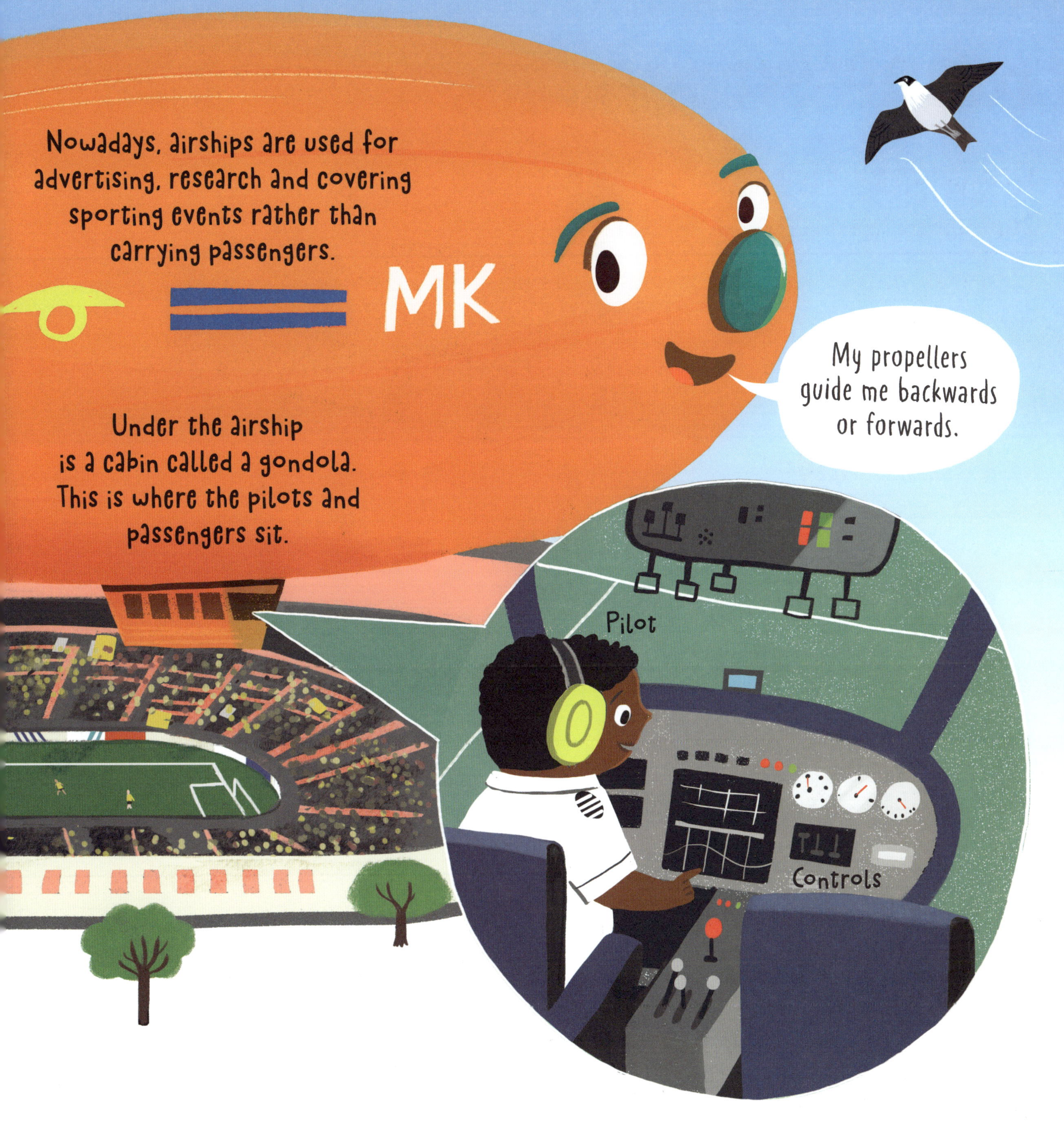

Nowadays, airships are used for advertising, research and covering sporting events rather than carrying passengers.
MK
Under the airship is a cabin called a gondola. This is where the pilots and passengers sit.
My propellers guide me backwards or forwards.
Pilot
Controls

Drone Power!

Drones are a type of aircraft that can fly without a pilot.

A drone can be used for all kinds of things, from taking photos of the Earth to delivering packages!

Some drones are remote-controlled by someone on the ground, while others are programmed by a computer.